Cinco de Mayo

I've got a fun activity for you on page 22!

M. C. Hall

Little World Holidays and Celebrations

ROURKE PUBLISHING

www.rourkepublishing.com

www.rourkepublishing.com

Photo credits: Michael Rubin/Shutterstock Images, cover; Gregory Bull/AP Images, 1, 14; Travel Bug/Shutterstock Images, 3; Michael Rubin/Shutterstock Images, 4; James Pauls/iStockphoto, 5; Camille Jossé/Fotolia, 6; Fotolia, 7; Red Line Editorial, Inc., 8; Jose Luis Magana/AP Images, 9; iStockphoto, 10; Eduardo Verdugo/AP Images, 11; Big Stock Photo, 12, 13; Nick M. Do/iStockphoto, 15; Lorena Altamirano/iStockphoto, 16; Danny E. Hooks/Shutterstock Images, 17; Travis Morisse/AP Images, 18; J. Helgason/Shutterstock Images, 19; Pétur Ásgeirsson/Shutterstock Images, 20; Juan David Ferrando Subero/Shutterstock Images, 21

Editor: Holly Saari

Cover and page design: Kazuko Collins

Content Consultant: Robert Con Davis-Undiano, PhD, Executive Director, *World Literature Today*, Neustadt Professor, Professor of English, University of Oklahoma

Library of Congress Cataloging-in-Publication Data

Hall, Margaret, 1947-
 Cinco de Mayo / M.C. Hall.
     p. cm. -- (Little world holidays and celebrations)
 Includes bibliographical references and index.
 ISBN 978-1-61590-243-9 (hard cover) (alk. paper)
 ISBN 978-1-61590-483-9 (soft cover)
 1. Cinco de Mayo (Mexican holiday)--History--Juvenile literature. 2. Mexico--Social life and customs--Juvenile literature.
I. Title.
 F1233.H18 2011
 394.262--dc22
                            2010009917

Rourke Publishing
Printed in the United States of America, North Mankato, Minnesota
033010
033010LP

www.rourkepublishing.com - rourke@rourkepublishing.com
Post Office Box 643328 Vero Beach, Florida 32964

What are these people doing?

They are celebrating Cinco de Mayo!

Cinco de Mayo means the Fifth of May in Spanish. Mexicans and Mexican-Americans celebrate the holiday on this day each year.

Cinco de Mayo started in Mexico. French
soldiers came to Mexico 150 years ago. They
wanted to take over the country.

Some Mexicans learned about the soldiers and wanted to stop them. They formed a group to fight the French.

On May 5 the French soldiers reached the town of Puebla. Mexican soldiers were waiting there. But there were twice as many French soldiers as Mexican soldiers.

Actors show how the Mexican soldiers were outnumbered.

There was a big **battle**. After a long day of fighting the Mexican soldiers won—even though they were outnumbered!

Mexico won the battle. But it did not win the war. One year later the French took over Mexico City for four years.

People act out the Battle of Puebla.

But the Battle of Puebla still made Mexicans proud. It showed that they would fight to stay free.

People wanted to remember the special day.
Cinco de Mayo became a holiday in Mexico.

Mexicans who moved to the United States also began celebrating the holiday. Today more people celebrate Cinco de Mayo in the United States than in Mexico!

Cinco de Mayo is a big **fiesta**. The holiday celebrates Mexico, Mexican **traditions**, and Mexican pride.

The Mexican flag is red, white, and green. So those are the colors of Cinco de Mayo.

Many people dress in traditional clothing. They play traditional music too. Mexican dancers twirl to the music.

Mexican food is a big part of Cinco de Mayo. People line up at stands to buy **tamales**, tacos, grilled corn, and beans. Everything tastes so good!

The **piñata** is another Cinco de Mayo tradition.
It is filled with candy and other treats.
Children take turns trying to hit the piñata.

At last the piñata breaks apart. The children hurry to collect the treats.

Many cities have parades to celebrate Cinco de Mayo. Bands march down the streets while playing music.

At last it is time for the fiesta to end. And that means fireworks!

Craft: Sound Shaker

What you need:
- Cardboard tube from a paper towel or toilet paper roll
- Clear tape
- Construction paper
- Crayons or markers
- Glue
- Scissors
- Uncooked rice or dried beans

1. Decorate one sheet of construction paper. Include pictures for Cinco de Mayo, like tacos or piñatas.

2. Glue the construction paper around the cardboard tube so your picture is showing.

3. On another piece of paper, trace the end of the cardboard tube twice. Cut out these two circles.

4. Tape one circle over one end of the tube. Pour the rice or beans into the tube until it is about half full. Tape the other circle onto the other end of the tube.

5. Shake your sound shaker to celebrate!

Glossary

battle (BAT-uhl): a fight between soldiers of different armies

fiesta (fee-ESS-tuh): a Spanish word that means "party"

piñata (peen-YAH-tuh): a hollow shape made from paper and paste and filled with candy

tamales (tuh-MAH-leez): a Mexican food of meat or beans in cornmeal that is wrapped in corn husks and steamed

traditions (truh-DISH-uhnz): things that are done in the same way for many years

Websites to Visit

holidays.kaboose.com/cinco-de-mayo/history/quick_facts.html

www.history.com/topics/cinco-de-mayo/videos#cinco-de-mayo

www.theholidayzone.com/cinco/cinco-de-mayo-songs.html

About the Author

M. C. Hall is a former elementary school teacher and an education consultant. As a freelance writer, she has authored teacher materials and more than 100 books for young readers. Hall lives and works in southeastern Massachusetts.